Solar
COOKING

Rob Waring, *Series Editor*

T0052134

HEINLE
CENGAGE Learning™

Australia • Brazil • Japan • Korea • Mexico • Singapore • Spain • United Kingdom • United States

Words to Know

This story starts in the U.S. cities of Sacramento [sækrəmɛntoʊ] and Borrego Springs [bɔreɪgoʊ sprɪŋz], California. It then moves on to villages in Africa and around the world.

 Solar Cooking. Read the sentences. Then complete the paragraph with the correct form of the underlined words.

Cardboard is very thick paper that is usually used for making boxes.
A cooker is a piece of equipment that is used to cook food.
Solar refers to something that is of or related to the sun.
A workshop is a meeting of people to learn more about a particular subject.

This story is about a way of using (1)_____ power to cook food. A group called 'Solar Cookers International' has developed a (2)_____ that is made of a thick paper. This paper, or (3)_____, is covered with a reflective material which uses the sun's light to cook food. (4)_____ are now being held around the world to teach people how to use the sun to cook food.

Villagers at a Solar Cooking Workshop

solar cooker

2

B **Solar Cookers Help People.** Read the paragraph. Then complete the definitions with the correct form of the words or phrases.

Developing countries have a number of significant problems. In some places, large areas are being deforested by people who need wood for energy. Charcoal and other fuels that people burn for cooking can cause health problems. The lack of safe drinking water and large number of waterborne diseases are also big issues. Unless water is pasteurized, it may carry diseases and make people ill. Microbiologist Bob Metcalf [mɛtkæf] and writer Eleanor Shimeall [ʃəmil] are teaching people how to fix these problems by using solar cookers in their everyday lives.

1. A scientist who studies very small living things, such as bacteria, is a m_____.

2. The cutting down of trees in large areas is called d_____.

3. C_____ is a hard, black substance that is burned for energy.

4. W_____ means to be carried or transferred by water.

5. A d_____ c_____ is a nation that is economically weak but growing.

6. F_____ are substances that release energy when burned.

7. To heat something at a controlled temperature in order to kill disease-causing elements is to p_____.

cardboard

reflective material

It's a cool but sunny day in Borrego Springs, California. As Eleanor Shimeall prepares to cook her meal, she opens the door and steps outside of her home. You see, this woman doesn't cook inside her kitchen—she cooks outdoors! She walks over to a strange-looking piece of equipment and opens a glass door to put in her bread. She then opens the lower part of another glass and wood construction and says, "I'm going to check on this chicken and rice and see how it's cooking." As she takes off the top of the pot, she can see that the dish is cooking nicely. "Ah, it's doing a good job," she says.

Shimeall's meal looks delicious; however, there's one remarkable thing about her cooking method. Unlike most people, she isn't using electricity, gas, charcoal, or wood to cook her food. Instead, Shimeall is using the sun to make her meal, and she's done it almost every day for more than 20 years. She cooks with solar power!

CD 3, Track 09

A Solar Cooker

A solar cooker is a type of **stove**[1] that needs only the light from the sun, or sunshine, to cook food. It can cook a delicious meal even if the air temperature is not very hot. Solar cookers can be used to cook meat, fish, grains, and vegetables. They can cook just about anything that can be cooked on a regular stove.

This method of cooking is becoming popular among people who are concerned about the environment. However, they aren't the only people interested in this unusual invention. In developing countries around the world, solar cookers have the potential to save lives. According to one expert, people around the world may soon not have enough traditional fuels. He explains in his own words, "With sunshine you have an alternative to fire. And that's important for two and a half billion people to learn about because they're running out of traditional fuels."

---

[1]**stove:** a piece of kitchen equipment, usually containing an oven, used to cook food

A Traditional Stove

Dr. Bob Metcalf is a microbiologist and a **founding member**[2] of Solar Cookers International, or SCI for short. He, along with Eleanor Shimeall and her husband, helped to create the small nonprofit organization which is based in Sacramento, California. For the last 15 years, SCI has promoted solar cooking around the world, especially in the developing countries of Africa.

The organization's goals focus primarily on two areas. They want to help stop the terrible deforestation which is occurring in some countries, and they want to make women's lives easier. The problem of deforestation is often due to the demand for trees to use as fuel. But how does an organization like SCI help women? How can women's lives be improved with solar cooking?

---

[2]**founding member:** one of the people who started an organization; the first in a group

Predict

Answer the questions using information that you know from reading to this point. Then check your answers on page 11.

1. What problems do women face with traditional cooking methods?

2. How can women's lives be improved with solar cooking? Explain two or three ideas.

Deforestation is a huge problem in some developing countries.

In order to help people better understand the issue, Dr. Metcalf describes the lifestyle of many women in parts of Africa. "They have to walk about two to three miles or so to collect wood," he says. "And then they have to tend the fire. And the smoke from that fire, it burns their eyes and **chokes their lungs**."[3]

According to the **World Health Organization**,[4] this indoor pollution has been linked to the deaths of two million women and children each year. With help from other human aid groups, Solar Cookers International has already trained more than 22,000 families. They have taught these families how to cook their traditional foods with the sun.

---

[3]**choke (one's) lungs:** cause breathing problems by blocking air ways in the breathing organs in the chest called the 'lungs'
[4]**World Health Organization (WHO):** an agency of the United Nations that works to improve global health conditions

But does solar cooking really work? Does it really cook food well? Solar Cookers International thinks so! The group organizes workshops on cooking with solar cookers. In these workshops, the women learn how to set up and use the solar cooking equipment. They also get a chance to actually prepare foods on the cookers. The women make a wide range of dishes including soups, rice, potatoes, and bread.

After a day of preparing the foods, the users are finally able to taste their 'solar-powered food'. "Oh, this is good," says one woman as she tries the food from a workshop. "It's very good," she continues, "The **consistency**[5] is good; the **texture**[6] is fine." She then concludes with a smile, "No problem!"

The fact that the solar cooker looks just like a cardboard box surprises many of the women. One of the cooks says, "We're all amazed that a cardboard box can cook." After each workshop, attendees are given their own **portable**[7] solar 'cook kits' to take home. They are then expected to use the kits to help them with their daily tasks. The simple cookers cost about five dollars, last almost two years, and work exactly like the more costly kits.

---

[5]**consistency:** the degree of thickness, softness, etc.
[6]**texture:** the way something feels according to sense of taste or touch
[7]**portable:** movable; capable of being carried or moved around

How does the solar cooker work? Dr. Metcalf explains: "Shiny things direct the sunshine onto a dark pot that then **absorbs**[8] the sunshine, and changes that light energy into heat energy." He then talks about how this heat energy becomes caught in the plastic bag or window that covers the pot in a solar cooker: "And heat energy doesn't get out of the clear plastic bag; it doesn't get out of the window."

Solar cooking is a simple yet brilliant idea that has several advantages. Not only is it a safe way to cook foods without traditional fuels, but SCI says that it's also an effective way of making water pure and safe to drink. These two capabilities make the solar cooker a major benefit for developing countries.

---

[8]**absorb:** slowly take in

Dr. Metcalf explains the importance of solar cookers in making water safe to consume. "Six thousand people a day are going to die of waterborne diseases in developing countries. If you heat water to 65° Celsius, 149° Fahrenheit, you can pasteurize water and make it safe to drink."

Solar Cookers International has developed a useful little measuring tool in order to help people to know when water is safe to drink. The measuring tool, which uses **wax**,[9] is designed to be placed in water that's on the cooker. Dr. Metcalf explains how the measuring tool works. "If the water gets hot enough to **melt**[10] this wax," he says, "the water has reached pasteurization temperatures." Basically, users can look at the simple clear container. If the wax is solid, the water is not safe. If the wax has melted, the people can drink the water and not get sick.

---

[9]**wax:** a soft substance used in candles
[10]**melt:** turn from a solid into something soft or liquid

Solar Cookers International has been very successful at making the lives of African women easier with their solar cooker workshops. Similar solar projects are now getting started in a number of countries. From Nepal to Nicaragua, solar cooking projects are helping people in nearly every country in the developing world. Some communities are even experimenting with solar cookers for large volumes of food. But SCI is not satisfied with just helping these people. Their goal is to increase the use of solar cookers everywhere.

Dr. Metcalf is aware of the importance of providing solar cooking technology to the places that need it the most. He explains in his own words. "Science is supposed to help and benefit all of mankind," he says, "and [we've] got something that is good science that could help two and a half billion people in the world." To this he then adds, "There's a great need [to share the] information that these things work." Dr. Metcalf wants to spread the news about the ease and safety of solar cooking. Hopefully someday soon, everyone will feel the way that one workshop attendee did. At the end of the training, she just smiled and said, "OK, solar cooker!"

Summarize

Imagine you are teaching one of the workshops.
Write or talk about the importance and the
benefits of the solar cooker.

After You Read

1. What does the word 'remarkable' mean in paragraph 2 on page 4?
    A. strange
    B. special
    C. serious
    D. standard

2. Which of the following does Eleanor Shimeall use to cook her food?
    A. wind
    B. gas
    C. sun
    D. wood

3. Why does solar cooking have the potential to save lives?
    A. It can replace disappearing fuels.
    B. It's safer than cooking with wood.
    C. It can make water safe to drink.
    D. all of the above

4. Which of the following is one of the main goals of Solar Cookers International?
    A. to make everyone in the world use solar cooking
    B. to teach people the benefits of alternative energy
    C. to give better lives to women in developing countries
    D. to stop the use of electric stoves

5. Which of the following is NOT a good heading for page 11?
    A. Wood Fires Bad for Health
    B. Millions Use Solar Cooking
    C. Traditional Fuel Takes Time
    D. Families Learn to Use New Stove

6. How many years does one solar cooker last?
    A. five
    B. one
    C. twenty-two
    D. two

7. One African woman expressed the view that the solar cooker:
   A. doesn't look like a stove
   B. doesn't make tasty food
   C. isn't small enough
   D. can't be used on a rainy day

8. What helps energy to stay in the solar cooker?
   A. a dark pot
   B. a cardboard box
   C. a shiny thing
   D. a clear plastic bag or window

9. What does 'it' refer to in paragraph 1 on page 16?
   A. waterborne disease
   B. Fahrenheit
   C. water
   D. a solar cooker

10. A measuring tool that uses wax _____ make water safe.
   A. doesn't
   B. helps to
   C. learns to
   D. tries to

11. What does Dr. Metcalf believe about the role of science in society?
   A. Science should be used to help people.
   B. Science doesn't support mankind enough.
   C. Society needs more organizations like his.
   D. Society should support science more.

12. What is the main purpose of the last paragraph?
   A. to introduce Dr. Metcalf's goals
   B. to show that people use solar cookers
   C. to give an example from Nepal
   D. to explain that the cookers are not successful yet

The History of
Solar Cooking

For most of human history, people did not cook their food. They simply ate it the way it was found. Thousands of years ago, people learned how to use fire for cooking purposes. However, humans have long been interested in using the heat from the sun to cook their food, as well. An ancient group of people called the Essenes lived in the northern part of Africa about 2,000 years ago. Records indicate that they heated thin pieces of bread on rocks that were warmed by the sun.

The first modern experiments in solar cooking began during the 1700s. At this time, glass was becoming more widely available and people began to use it for windows. It soon became clear that when the sun passed through a glass window into a closed room, the air in the room became warmer.

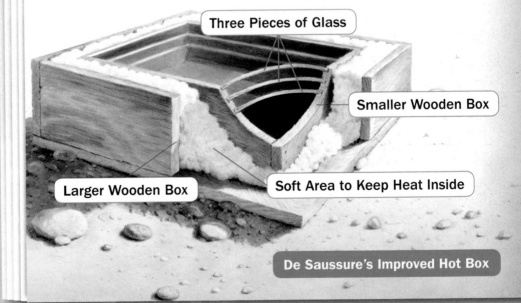

Three Pieces of Glass

Smaller Wooden Box

Larger Wooden Box

Soft Area to Keep Heat Inside

De Saussure's Improved Hot Box

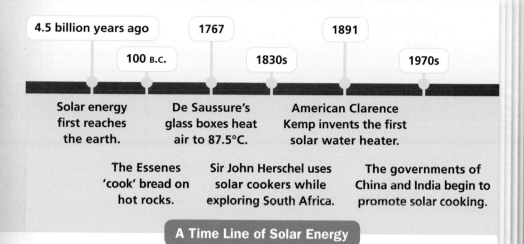

| 4.5 billion years ago | 1767 | 1891 |
| 100 B.C. | 1830s | 1970s |

Solar energy first reaches the earth.

De Saussure's glass boxes heat air to 87.5°C.

American Clarence Kemp invents the first solar water heater.

The Essenes 'cook' bread on hot rocks.

Sir John Herschel uses solar cookers while exploring South Africa.

The governments of China and India begin to promote solar cooking.

A Time Line of Solar Energy

In the 1760s a French-Swiss scientist, Horace de Saussure, became interested in why this happened and how much heat could be produced this way. In 1767, he conducted an experiment which measured the temperature changes in boxes as they were heated by the sun.

De Saussure's first experiment involved a set of five small glass boxes, each one placed inside of the other. The largest box was 12 inches by 12 inches and the smallest box was 2 inches by 2 inches. He placed the boxes on a black wooden table. He used a black surface because he knew it would hold the heat of the sun rather than reflecting it away. After several hours, he checked the temperatures in the boxes. The outer box was coolest and the smallest box in the center was warmest. The temperature in the inner box was 87.5°C*. De Saussure had placed some fruits in this container and found that the fruits were actually cooked by the heat in the box. Later he built a more efficient heat box using wood and glass and was able to raise the temperature to 109°C. This is well above the boiling point of water, which is 100°C. This improved cooker later became known as a 'hot box' and was the basis for many further solar experiments.

CD 3, Track 10

Word Count: 361
Time: _____

*See page 24 for a metric conversion chart

Vocabulary List

absorb (15)
cardboard (2, 3, 12)
charcoal (3, 4)
choke (one's) lungs (11)
consistency (12)
cooker (2, 3, 7, 8, 11, 12, 15, 16, 18, 19)
deforest (3, 8)
developing country (3, 7, 8, 15, 16, 18)
founding member (8)
fuel (3, 7, 8)
melt (16)
microbiologist (3, 8)
pasteurize (3, 16)
portable (12)
solar (2, 3, 4, 7, 8, 9, 11, 12, 15, 16, 18, 19)
stove (7)
texture (12)
waterborne (3, 16)
wax (16)
workshop (2, 12, 18, 19)

Metric Conversion Chart

Area
1 hectare = 2.471 acres

Length
1 centimeter = .394 inches
1 meter = 1.094 yards
1 kilometer = .621 miles

Temperature
0° Celsius = 32° Fahrenheit

Volume
1 liter = 1.057 quarts

Weight
1 gram = .035 ounces
1 kilogram = 2.2 pounds